FIRESIDE SE[RIES]

Volume 1, No. 3

Ramtha

Forgotten
Gods Waking Up

FORGOTTEN GODS WAKING UP

Copyright © 2001 JZK, Inc.

Cover illustration by Carmel Bartz

ISBN # 1-57873-058-9

JZK Publishing,
A Division of JZK, Inc.

P.O. Box 1210
Yelm, Washington 98597
360.458.5201
800.347.0439
www.ramtha.com
www.jzkpublishing.com

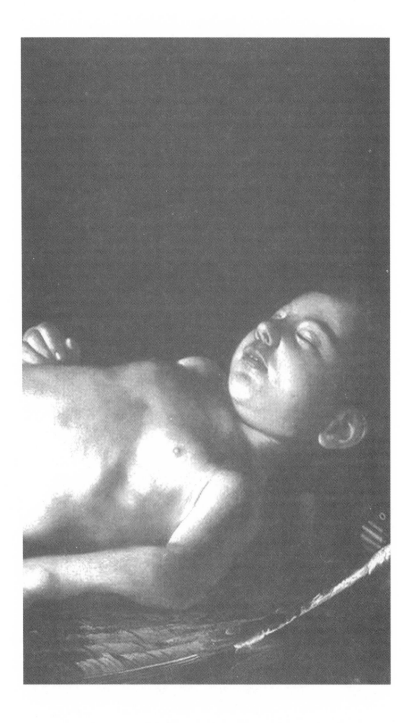

These series of teachings are designed for all the students of the Great Work who love the teachings of the Ram.

It is suggested that you create an ideal learning environment for study and contemplation.

Light your fireplace and get cozy. Have your wine and fine tobacco. Prepare yourself. Open your mind to learn and be genius.

Foreword to the New Edition

The Fireside Series Collection Library is an ongoing library of the hottest topics of interest taught by Ramtha. These series of teachings are designed for all the students of the Great Work who love the teachings of the Ram. This library collection is also intended as a continuing learning tool for the students of Ramtha's School of Enlightenment and for everyone interested and familiar with Ramtha's teachings.

In the last three decades Ramtha has continuously and methodically deepened and expanded his exposition of the nature of reality and its practical application through various disciplines. It is assumed by the publisher that the reader has attended a Beginning Retreat or workshop through Ramtha's School of Enlightenment or is at least familiar with Ramtha's instruction to his beginning class of students. This required information for beginning students is found in *Ramtha: A Beginner's Guide to Creating Reality*, revised and expanded ed. (Yelm: JZK Publishing, a division of JZK, Inc., 2000), and in *Ramtha: Creating Personal Reality*, Video ed. (Yelm: JZK Publishing, a division of JZK, Inc., 1998).

We have included in the Fireside Series a glossary of some of the basic concepts used by Ramtha so the reader can become familiarized with these teachings. We have also included a brief introduction of Ramtha by JZ Knight that describes how all this began. Enjoy your learning and contemplation.

CONTENTS

FIGURES

Introduction to Ramtha
By JZ Knight

"In other words, his whole point of focus is to come here and to teach you to be extraordinary."

You don't have to stand for me. My name is JZ Knight and I am the rightful owner of this body, and welcome to Ramtha's school, and sit down. Thank you.

So we will start out by saying that Ramtha and I are two different people, beings. We have a common reality point and that is usually my body. I am a lot different than he is. Though we sort of look the same, we really don't look the same.

What do I say? Let's see. All of my life, ever since I was a little person, I have heard voices in my head and I have seen wonderful things that to me in my life were normal. And I was fortunate enough to have a family or a mother who was a very psychic human being, who sort of never condemned what it was that I was seeing. And I had wonderful experiences all my life, but the most important experience was that I had this deep and profound love for God, and there was a part of me that understood what that was. Later in my life I went to church and I tried to understand God from the viewpoint of religious doctrine and had a lot of difficulty with that because it was sort of in conflict with what I felt and what I knew.

Ramtha has been a part of my life ever since I was born, but I didn't know who he was and I didn't know what he was, only that there was a wonderful force that walked with me, and when I was in trouble — and had a lot of pain in my life growing up — that I always had extraordinary experiences with this being who would talk to me. And I could hear him as clearly as I can hear you if we were to have a conversation. And he helped me to understand a lot of things in my life that were sort of beyond the normal scope of what someone would give someone as advice.

It wasn't until 1977 that he appeared to me in my kitchen on a Sunday afternoon as I was making pyramids with my husband at that time, because we were into dehydrating food and we were into hiking and backpacking and all that stuff. And so I put one of these ridiculous things on my head, and at the other end of my kitchen this wonderful apparition appeared that was seven feet tall and glittery and beautiful and stark. You just don't expect at 2:30 in the afternoon that this is going to appear in your kitchen. No one is ever prepared for that. And so Ramtha at that time really made his appearance known to me.

The first thing I said to him — and I don't know where this comes from — was that "You are so beautiful. Who are you?"

And he has a smile like the sun. He is extraordinarily handsome. And he said, "My name is Ramtha the Enlightened One, and I have come to help you over the ditch." Being the simple person that I am, my immediate reaction was to look at the floor because I thought maybe something had happened to the floor, or the bomb was being dropped; I didn't know.

And it was that day forward that he became a constant in my life. And during the year of 1977 a lot of interesting things happened, to say the least. My two younger children at that time got to meet Ramtha and got to experience some incredible phenomena, as well as my husband.

Later that year, after teaching me and having some difficulty telling me what he was and me understanding, one day he said to me, "I am going to send you a runner that will bring you a set of books, and you read them because then you will know what I am." And those books were called the *Life and Teaching of the Masters of the Far East* (DeVorss & Co. Publishers, 1964). And so I read them and I began to understand that Ramtha was one of those beings, in a way. And that sort of took me out of the are-you-the-devil-or-are-you-God sort of category that was plaguing me at the time.

And after I got to understand him, he spent long, long

moments walking into my living room, all seven feet of this beautiful being making himself comfortable on my couch, sitting down and talking to me and teaching me. And what I didn't realize at that particular time was he already knew all the things I was going to ask and he already knew how to answer them. But I didn't know that he knew that.

So he patiently since 1977 has dealt with me in a manner by allowing me to question not his authenticity but things about myself as God, teaching me, catching me when I would get caught up in dogma or get caught up in limitation, catching me just in time and teaching me and walking me through that. And I always said, "You know, you are so patient. You know, I think it is wonderful that you are so patient." And he would just smile and say that he is 35,000 years old, what else can you do in that period of time? So it wasn't really until about ten years ago that I realized that he already knew what I was going to ask and that is why he was so patient. But as the grand teacher that he is, he allowed me the opportunity to address these issues in myself and then gave me the grace to speak to me in a way that was not presumptuous but in a way, as a true teacher would, that would allow me to come to realizations on my own.

Channeling Ramtha since late 1979 has been an experience, because how do you dress your body for — Ram is seven feet tall and he wears two robes that I have always seen him in. Even though they are the same robe, they are really beautiful so you never get tired of seeing them. The inner robe is snow white and goes all the way down to where I presume his feet are, and then he has an overrobe that is beautiful purple. But you should understand that I have really looked at the material on these robes and it is not really material. It is sort of like light. And though the light has a transparency to them, there is an understanding that what he is wearing has a reality to it.

Ramtha's face is cinnamon-colored skin, and that is the best way I can describe it. It is not really brown and it is not really white and it is not really red; it is sort of a blending of that. And he has very deep black eyes that can look into you and you know you are being looked into. He has eyebrows that look like wings of a bird that come high on his brow. He has a very square jaw and a beautiful mouth, and when he smiles you know that you are in heaven. He has long, long hands, long fingers that he uses very eloquently to demonstrate his thought.

Well, imagine then how after he taught me to get out of my body by actually pulling me out and throwing me in the tunnel, and hitting the wall of light, bouncing back, and realizing my kids were home from school and I just got through doing breakfast dishes, that getting used to missing time on this plane was really difficult, and I didn't understand what I was doing and where I was going. So we had a lot of practice sessions.

You can imagine if he walked up to you and yanked you right out of your body and threw you up to the ceiling and said now what does that view look like, and then throwing you in a tunnel — and perhaps the best way to describe it is it is a black hole into the next level — and being flung through this tunnel and hitting this white wall and having amnesia. And you have to understand, I mean, he did this to me at ten o'clock in the morning and when I came back off of the white wall it was 4:30. So I had a real problem in trying to adjust with the time that was missing here. So we had a long time in teaching me how to do that, and it was fun and frolic and absolutely terrifying at moments.

But what he was getting me ready to do was to teach me something that I had already agreed to prior to this incarnation, and that my destiny in this life was not just to marry and to have children and to do well in life but to overcome the adversity to let what was previously planned happen, and that happening including an extraordinary consciousness, which he is.

Trying to dress my body for Ramtha was a joke. I didn't

know what to do. The first time we had a channeling session I wore heels and a skirt and, you know, I thought I was going to church. So you can imagine, if you have got a little time to study him, how he would appear dressed up in a business suit with heels on, which he has never walked in in his life.

But I guess the point that I want to tell you is that it is really difficult to talk to people — and perhaps someday I will get to do that with you, and understanding that you have gotten to meet Ramtha and know his mind and know his love and know his power — and how to understand that I am not him, and though I am working diligently on it, that we are two separate beings and that when you talk to me in this body, you are talking to me and not him. And sometimes over the past decade or so, that has been a great challenge to me in the public media because people don't understand how it is possible that a human being can be endowed with a divine mind and yet be separate from it.

So I wanted you to know that although you see Ramtha out here in my body, it is my body, but he doesn't look anything like this. But his appearance in the body doesn't lessen the magnitude of who and what he is. And you should also know that when we do talk, when you start asking me about things that he said, I may not have a clue about what you are talking about because when I leave my body in a few minutes, I am gone to a whole other time and another place that I don't have cognizant memory of. And however long he spends with you today, to me that will maybe be about five minutes or three minutes, and when I come back to my body, this whole time of this whole day has passed and I wasn't a part of it. And I didn't hear what he said to you and I don't know what he did out here. When I come back, my body is exhausted and it is hard to get up the stairs sometimes to change to make myself more presentable for what the day is bringing me, or what is left of the day.

You should also understand as beginning students, one thing that became really obvious over the years, that he has shown me a lot of wonderful things that I suppose people who have never gotten to see them couldn't even dream of in their wildest dreams. And I have seen the twenty-third universe and I have met extraordinary beings and I have seen life come and go. I have watched generations be born and live and pass in a matter of moments. I have been exposed to historical events to help me to understand better what it was I needed to know. I have been allowed to walk beside my body in other lifetimes and watch how I was and who I was, and I have been allowed to see the other side of death. So these are cherished and privileged opportunities that somewhere in my life I earned the right to have them in my life. To speak of them to other people is, in a way, disenchanting because it is difficult to convey to people who have never been to those places what it is. And I try my best as a storyteller to tell them and still fall short of it.

But I know that the reason that he works with his students the way that he does is because also Ramtha never wants to overshadow any of you. In other words, his whole point of focus is to come here and to teach you to be extraordinary; he already is. And it is not about him producing phenomena. If he told you he was going to send you runners, you are going to get them big time. It is not about him doing tricks in front of you; that is not what he is. Those are tools of an avatar that is still a guru that needs to be worshiped, and that is not the case with him.

So what will happen is he will teach you and cultivate you and allow you to create the phenomenon, and you will be able to do that. And then one day when you are able to manifest on cue and you are able to leave your body and you are able to love, when it is to the human interest impossible to do that, one day he will walk right out here in your life because you are ready to share what he is. And what he is is simply what you are going to become. And until then he is diligent, patient, all-knowing, and all-understanding of everything that we need to know in order to learn to be that.

And the one thing I can say to you is that if you are interested in what you have heard in his presentation, and you are starting to love him even though you can't see him, that is a good sign because it means that what was important in you was your soul urging you to unfold in this lifetime. And it may be against your neuronet. Your personality can argue with you and debate with you, but you are going to learn that that sort of logic is really transparent when the soul urges you onto an experience.

And I can just say that if this is what you want to do, you are going to have to exercise patience and focus and you are going to have to do the work. And the work in the beginning is very hard. But if you have the tenacity to stay with it, then one day I can tell you that this teacher is going to turn you inside out. And one day you will be able to do all the remarkable things that in myth and legend that the masters that you have heard of have the capacity to do. You will be able to do them because that is the journey. And ultimately that ability is singularly the reality of a God awakening in human form.

Now that is my journey and it has been my journey all of my life. And if it wasn't important and if it wasn't what it was, I certainly wouldn't be living in oblivion most of the year for the sake of having a few people come and have a New Age experience. This is far greater than a New Age experience. And I should also say that it is far more important than the ability to meditate or the ability to do yoga. It is about changing consciousness all through our lives on every point and to be able to unhinge and unlimit our minds so that we can be all we can be.

You should also know that what I have learned is we can only demonstrate what we are capable of demonstrating. And if you would say, well, what is blocking me from doing that, the only block that we have is our lack to surrender, our ability to surrender, our ability to allow, and our ability to support ourself even in the face of our own neurological or neuronet doubt. If you can support yourself through doubt, then you will make the breakthrough because that is the only block that stands in your way. And one day you are going to do all these things and get to see all the things that I have seen and been allowed to see.

So I just wanted to come out here and show you that I exist and that I love what I do and that I hope that you are learning from this teacher and, more importantly, I hope you continue with it.

— *JZ Knight*

You Are the Forgotten Gods

Greetings, my beautiful masters. I salute you from the Lord God of my being to the Lord God of your being. Welcome. So be it.

I Ramtha the Enlightened One, that which is termed, as it were, Lord of the Wind, of that which is termed ascended Master, of that which is termed servant unto Christ, to that which is termed God/man realized, to that which is termed Lord of my era, I speak this hour and say unto you salutations unto you who are Gods.

And unto you who awaken to become Gods, I say this, the following: that what you shall hear in the days that follow this tribute shall be that which is termed words of truth that unlock the prison of that which is termed your forgetfulness and wake you up. I say to you that these words and indeed these teachings I manifest straightaway, for we have reached to that which is termed the circle that I cannot enter. We are entering that which is termed the momentum that has no words, and that which I teach to you I send runners straightaway that you will know this truth, for this is the year of the great awakening. And thereby I say, to all of my words, they shall manifest straightaway and indeed in their manifestation they shall be truth, that you shall know that God lives within you and that which has been taught to you is that which is termed the truth and the kingdom of heaven. So say I from the Lord God of my being, Ramtha the Enlightened One. So be it. To two hundred years and everlasting life. So be it.

Now let me begin by saying to you, my beautiful, illustrious participants, first I want you to know before we begin that I love you and that you are the people of the Great Ram. And more important than even that is that you are indeed that which is termed the teachings called the forgotten Gods and you are waking up, and this is the time that you have set aside in your year. You have left your families, your environments, you have left that which is termed your commitments, you have left your image, or at least tried to, and you have made that which is termed your pilgrimage to this holy place. And you should understand then that you have to your credit a commitment in your life to your spiritual evolution. And if what you have learned here was not fruitful in your life, you most certainly indeed would not have come back, and you would not have spent your money, nor would you have set aside your time for that which is termed your own spiritual growth. And that I say to you is your credit to that which is termed not only who you are, but that is a commitment to the forgotten Gods that we are dedicating this grand and marvelous Retreat to. So be it.

As you have been taught, there are always multiple potentials that exist every moment, and that if we lay into the future on how we want to create our life, when you are a master you can see all the potentials and you can choose the one that is the one that you wish to walk, that you wish to experience. Well, there were many days about this day that has already happened, and the one that I have chosen that links up with many other potentials is what is going to happen today, and I know exactly how to conduct it.

Attitude is everything. We are not here to be better bodies. We are not here to be better taste buds. We are not here to wear solid white garments that are not going to get stained. We are not here for any of those things. And we are not here today so that we can hurry up and get it over with so that you can hurry up and get it over with. Do you understand? These are all the arguments of the personality.

I speak this hour as that which is termed Ramtha the Enlightened One. I am that which is termed the Lord of the Wind. I am that which is termed my ascended being. I am that which is termed greater than my humanity. I am indeed

the God of my times. I speak to you this hour. Of that
which I am, I am a servant unto the God within your being.
I am a lover of the Christ, which is God/human realized.
Unto that end I say this hour and command my law that
swiftly that which is taught this day shall it be learned and
absorbed by you, and that my words, that they manifest
straightaway in your life and that that manifestation then
bear the manifestation of truth to you that you may see
that what is taught to you this day is to bring you nearer to
God, to the unfoldment of Christhood that is God/man,
God/woman realized, the God in human form. And I say
this day that all that is taught shall be realized and that
which is realized shall free you from your sickness, for I
command it so, shall destroy your illness, for I command it
so, and shall free you from your past, for I command it so,
that you may know the true joy and indeed the true bliss of
the God that I am and indeed the God that you are, and
that we are rulers of the new kingdom rather than the
holders of the old. So say I, Ramtha the Enlightened One.
And may you live uninterrupted for two hundred years, and
may we recall in a great convention of celebration this fine
day in remembrance. So here is to you, two hundred years
of life without death. So be it. To life.

If you are sincere, I want you to say:

I, the Observer,
accept this knowledge
and open my life
to the re-formation,
the changes
this knowledge shall bring
straightaway.
So be it.
To two hundred years.

Sit down. Break bread and cheese with one another,
foodstuffs. Now we are going to begin.

THE SERIOUS STUDENT OF THE GREAT WORK

If you are a serious student of the Great Work — and, by God, look what you have gone through in order to maintain this status — then hereto as we drink together and take bread together, that every moment that you are here that we are engaging and growing in our spiritual self. When you return, your personality is going to have had a crucial blow. Be certain and unafraid that those of you who maintain that who you are is who you are — your personality, what you own, who you are with, where you live, what you have, what you do not have, your victimization, your self-imposed importance — all of that will maintain itself. Do not worry. You are not going to lose what you do not want to lose.

Now but this is our annual union, isn't it? This is to say why would I pay this gold? Why would I set aside this time? Why would I leave my mother and my father, my sister and my brother, my husband, my wife, my lover? Why would I leave my employer? Why would I leave that which is termed the land of my culture? Why would you do all of that to come here and wipe the war paint off of your face and set aside your fine linens and your fine silks and take up the garment of this school? Why would you come here and lay behind your image? People who are involved in the image to degrees are not here. And if that isn't poignant in your life, I cannot give you a greater teaching than to say that those who are sharing the path of this journey are the ones that are here. Those that are not involved in the journey are those that are involved in their looks, their body, their appearance, their status in life. And I can tell you, go to the graveyard and you will find the meaningfulness of such a choice.

So where was I? I was at this point of saying to you that those of you — and look around you — who are here, you do not judge them. They came here and put aside all of the things that you thought were so important in your life; they have put aside those things in their life to be here, to come and to learn. I swear to you, my beloved people, the days that we are together, if you count all of the days in your calendar year, are so small in relation to the ingrained personality for the rest of the year. And when you are here and we are meeting, I am meeting from another place, you are meeting from other places, and we come together in a convention. And in this convention you are the student and you lay aside everything, and I want you to. The more you do that, the greater your growth.

I want you to be naked in this. And you say to those around you who would seduce you, you say to those around you who would use you and abuse you, you say to your own personality that cannot quite forget leaving behind what you have left behind to be here, you say to it, "Look, this is the time I dedicate to my God that has made my life and my fickle image possible. It is a small tribute to the glory of the one who breathed into me the breath of life, for this is my time spent in loving and learning and allowing God in my life, that I too may be a Christ one day." It is a small request in the light of all the rest of the days that you are not even here.

So, you are together because you went through the Boktau and you have made these changes. Now I want to tell you that this year in your time and counting we are nearing the end of that which is termed my mission. And therefore for all the times in your life that you were unimpeccable outside of this school, and for all the moments that you were unimpeccable, and for all the moments that you lived your image and not your God, and for all of the moments that you set aside what I have taught you for that which is termed the support of a body's face, a body's muscles, a body's youth, that you have set aside goodness and God and power for the sake of what you look like in the mirror, for all of the thousands upon thousands of words that have issued forth from this body, of all of the truths that have been demonstrated flagrantly in the face of that which is termed your personality, of all the miracles that you have done, of all of the coincidences, of all of the moments of serendipity, of all of the moments to which you had prophetic dreams, of all of the moments that like magic what you thought manifested, those are all bearing fruit. And you remember this, from this tree and this great school and the selection of the soul in this life to make this the life that says "I have seen everywhere. I have done everything. What I have never done is to see the twenty-third universe, I have never resurrected the dead, I have never healed the crippled, I have never healed myself and set it free. And indeed I could speak those concepts intellectually. Why, I have even been renowned as being an orator of that which is termed the word of a God, but put me to that which is termed the fire and I could not do anything."

This is the life that says, all of these concepts were always hinted at. They were always written about. They were prophesied. The irritants in every generation are the prophets. Indeed the irritants in every generation are the geniuses. The irritants in every generation are the healers. The irritants in every generation are that which calls out from the deserts and says I don't care how beautiful you think you are, you are going to die. And I don't care how rich you think you are, you cannot take it to the kingdom of heaven. And I don't care how beautiful you think your body is — and I don't care how much you think that you are missing life and you might as well live it now — the blind always fall in the ditch, which means that a ditch represents hell in the terms of that which is termed Hebraic ancient text. The ditch represents the open grave that was always called hell. And I don't care how much you think you have got going for you, you have nothing going for you if you do not have in this lifetime that which beckons to you a source of consciousness that beseeches you to wake up, and this is the opportunity for waking up. And when we come together near the end of my mission I can say to you, what have I not told you, and indeed what have I not taught you, and who has stood in the way of all of these teachings to the miraculous? It is your personality. It is your self-proclaimed importance. You think you are so important, but all of that importance has denied the vision of the greater importance, which is that which is termed the spiritual self, the true self.

You do not find the true self when you keep celebrating the image in its life because I can tell you there is nothing you haven't done, there is nothing you haven't seen, there is nothing you haven't lived. And the day that you realize that what you haven't experienced — raising the dead, healing the sick, resurrecting and making new the bones of the crippled, being able to walk with masters, being able to align oneself with the twenty-third universe, that is what you have never done — and the day that you say that is the day that that which is really important in you will rise up. And that truth is called the Observer that makes the path of the new life. The personality never makes the path of the new life because it only knows how to re-create the path of the old.

Only the Observer Knows the Way

It takes the Observer to lay down the new life, that the body and that which is termed the personality are thus defined in the echelons of exploration and that which is termed evaluating that experience through evolution. It takes the Observer to know about the twenty-third universe, and it takes the Observer in order to heal one who is crippled, and it takes the Observer to that which is termed make perfect life, and it takes the Observer to reverse time in the body, and it takes the Observer to manifest the kingdom of heaven, for what say you that the personality knows indeed that the Observer does not? The personality only knows its small and meaningless sensual feelings that reassure it physical life every day, that it is living life to the fullest. But I say to you, how many days and how many centuries and how many lives do you need to be sensual to the first three seals?

And if this then be that which is termed the personality, then I say to you that the Observer is that which is extraordinary beyond that. And this school, and it is reunion, is about bringing closer before the end of my teaching you to the Observer — that is the only one that knows the true path ahead of you — for I am the Hierophant that will initiate you into God and I am the one that will teach you to surrender to it. But it will be that which is termed your own God that will take you to these far-flung places and enable for you to do the remarkable that the personality, for all of your intellectual glory, could never, ever accomplish even in ten million lifetimes.

Let's have a drink. To the glory of the kingdom of heaven that is in all of you. To the glory of God that is in all of you. To that which is termed the Christ, the epic of God/man and God/woman realized. To that which is termed all of you who near that which is termed the nucleus from the circumference of life. So be it.

Now so what am I saying to you? I am saying to you this school is not for naught, that everything I have taught you everyone in this audience has done. You have healed sickness. You have had prophetic dreams. You have found your card in the field.[1] How many of you have done that? So be it. And how many of you have prophetic dreams, prophetic dreams? So be it. How many of you have healed your body of sickness? So be it. How many of you have healed another? So be it. How many of you have manifested the dreams of your conscious reality? So be it. How many

---

1 Discipline of Fieldwork℠. See glossary.

of you have developed sending-and-receiving and can accurately read the mind of another? So be it. How many of you know the truth that consciousness and energy creates the nature of reality? So be it. Surely the greatest masters that ever lived could count these miracles amongst themselves. So what does that say about you? That you keep company in consciousness to the greatest teachers that have ever lived.

Now surely you understand that never did I ever come to you, in as long as you can remember, that I was not passionate about life and indeed that I did not bring to you and extol to you the God that you are. For as long as you have heard me speak, to whom have I glorified in every talk? It has been the God that you are. For twenty years in your time and counting, the greatest message is that you are God and the mission was to deliver that message to you. For twenty years I have been telling you the truth.

THE BIOLOGY OF THE PERSONALITY: A REVIEW

Now there is a group that have been studying before you ever arrived here. And they stayed because this was more important to them than their holidays and it was more important to them than their life. And they have stayed here to uncover what the most remarkable teaching yet has been about and that is to understand the Observer in that which is termed direct opposition to the personality and to understand that the human existence is made of two levels of consciousness, Point Zero and mirror consciousness. Now, easy to remember, for I have repeated it numerous times.

Now this year, in that which is termed nineteen hundred — according to which calendar? Is it the Julian calendar or the Gregorian calendar? Well, according to one, we are already in Armageddon, and according to the other we are only five years behind. So I suppose that both calendars are really relative to the personality and to God.

This group have studied the biology of the personality. When I say biology, they have studied emotions in regard to actual chemistry in the body, and indeed they have studied the personality is nothing more than a neuronet connected to the body by the form of chemicals. And those chemicals are called neuropeptides in the body, distributed through that which is termed the limbic system of the brain. And the limbic system of the brain throughout the body represents in that which is termed the ganglia of nerves on the spine exactly where the seven seals are located in the body.[2]

This group has studied the biology of the personality, the actual biology of stress, the biology of limited thinking,

2 See Fig. A in the glossary: *The Seven Seals: Seven Levels of Consciousness in the Human Body.*

the biology of the image, the biology of sexuality, the biology of victimization, the biology of that which is termed tyranny. They have actually already studied that. They are already ahead of you. And in that they came to clearly define red in the rainbow,[3] analogically speaking, as that which is termed that which they were. Analogical is being that which is, and you have all been the personality. We have already learned the physiology and indeed the neurology and indeed the biochemistry of the personality that you think is the truth.[4]

FIG. 1: CELLULAR BIOLOGY AND THE THOUGHT CONNECTION: FEEDBACK LOOP OF REDEMPTION/ADDICTION OR EVOLUTION

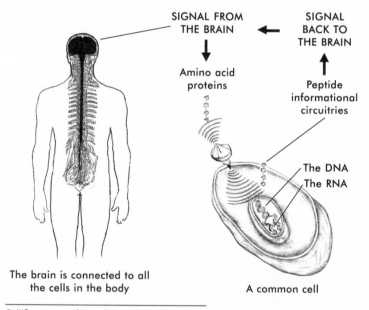

SIGNAL FROM THE BRAIN

SIGNAL BACK TO THE BRAIN

Amino acid proteins

Peptide informational circuitries

The DNA
The RNA

The brain is connected to all the cells in the body

A common cell

---

3 "If you are the color red in the rainbow, what is the one color you will not see? That means you are analogically red. When you become this to Infinite Unknown, then you cannot describe it until you are separate from it. You simply are it. Get it?" *Ramtha, Unfolding Dimensional Aspects of Self,* Tape 308 ed. (Yelm: Ramtha Dialogues, 1991).
4 See *Who Are We Really?* Fireside Series, Vol. 2, No. 5 (Yelm: JZK Publishing, a division of JZK, Inc., 2002).

And they have already learned about that which is termed the actual chemical hormones and neuropeptides and proteins that actually carry the signature of not only stress, and then the addiction through their opiate receptors of redemption from that stress. They have found that addiction is not limited to that which is termed narcotics and alcohol but true addiction is to that which is termed stress and indeed its redemption thereof. And they have learned that their whole life and their emotional body were about incorporating and maintaining stress, and then for the sake of being redeemed of that stress in the form of that which is termed the neuropeptides in the brain that bring about noradrenaline, or that which is termed the high in the body that is the natural opiate of the body — They have learned that addicts are not those who take drugs and alcohol and, although they are, that the greatest addicts are victims.

They have learned to step aside from being red and to see their life controlled as a personality and image through the neuronet, the brain's neurological/chemical/electrical connection to that which is termed the biology of every individual cell. They have learned that. They have learned about that which is termed the DNA and the RNA and going through to create their own peptides that allow in the form of amino acid chains communication that causes the cells to replicate and indeed to mirror exactly what the personality is. So there is proof that your attitudes you wear in the form of a physical body.

True Nature of the Voices in Our Head

Moreover, they learned that then the voices that they hear in their head that they attribute to being a spiritual being, the voices that they hear talking to them that they think is some celestial being out here, are nothing more than the voices of their personality chemically reacting in the brain. And they have learned to listen to the voices of that which is termed the senators that represent the seven quadrants of the body, representing the cells that really make up the whole mind/body complex, thereby identifying chemically the emotion. They have learned to see that. And they have learned that the voices that talk to them in their head are the voices of their emotions. They have learned to listen, and the greatest teaching they have learned in ten days was who is listening to the voices. Who is listening? Now we begin to file in upon the concept of God within, because who is listening to the chemical/biochemical personality, genetic personality? Who is listening to the voices in the brain? Then we have isolated God. We have isolated that which is termed the divine, and that we have called the Observer.

Fig. 2: The Neuronet Firing and Producing Thought

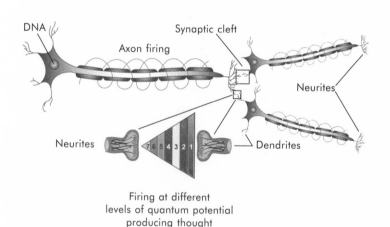

Firing at different
levels of quantum potential
producing thought

These people have been working with the Observer that can bypass the body completely to collapse the wave energy of reality of subatomic quantum physics into particle manifestation. They have found that God need not have that which is termed the body, that God only needs to become the Observer and that in the Observer, the brain presents the Observer the hologram of the thought, and without ever feeling it emotionally that the Observer, observing the brain's pictorial holographic image of a thought, can manifest it straightaway without it ever being felt emotionally.

FIG. 3: THE OBSERVER COLLAPSING ENERGY INTO PARTICLE REALITY

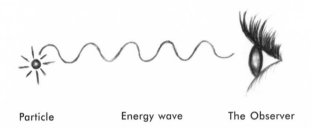

Particle   Energy wave   The Observer

They are beginning to isolate the Observer and indeed enter to that which is termed a realm that is a teaching without words. It is the holiest of holies. When one moves into becoming analogically the Observer, there is no path and indeed there are no words that teach us save only that this then is the kingdom of heaven. And these people have learned to discern the ancient teachings.

The Teachings of Yeshua ben Joseph

When Yeshua ben Joseph said to that which is termed his followers, "I am the son of the living God" — And when did he speak as the son of God and when did he speak as that which is termed the son of man? And why in that which is termed ancient literature did Yeshua, Jesus of Nazareth, speak at some times — when he said "I am speaking as the son of man" — why did he speak as the son of man and when indeed did he speak as the son of God? Because Yeshua ben Joseph was acknowledging in that which is termed his life — heir apparent to that which is termed the kingdom of Judea, the Hebrew people and all of its tribes — he was acknowledging that when he speaks "I am now speaking as a human" and then he would say "I am speaking as the son of man," and yet when he spoke from his divinity, from that which is termed his Observer, he would speak, as it were, and he would say, "Behold, I am speaking as the Father within me, for the Father within me hath given me this to speak. And indeed it is the Father within me that hath made this possible. It is not me."

And when he says that, he is saying, "It is not my personality that made this miracle, because it is impossible for it to make a miracle. Its only domain is emotion and feeling. That is its total domain. So when I say to you I speak to you as the son of that which is termed my Father's house, I am speaking to you as a personality, as a human being. But when I speak to you as that which is termed the son of God, I am speaking to you as the Observer that says that whatsoever I say in the name of the Observer, so it is done, not only in heaven but on Earth."

And he said to those that followed him, "We are children of two parents. We are the children of the humanity, of our father's loins and our mother's womb, and we are also the children of that which begat us into human form. We are also the children of God. We speak from two thrones. We are dual rulers. And what say you?" say he. "Who do you rule from? Do you rule your life from your emotions or do you rule it from that which is unemotional called the Observer?"

And these people learned how to differentiate creating their life from their emotional body from that which is termed their God body, and that which they create from their God body they are not emotionally in turmoil but are without emotion. And in that they do command the manifestations straightaway.

Our Divine Parent, Point Zero

So what am I saying? Then I am saying this: The greatest teaching that could ever be delivered to the peoples of this Earth, called Terra, is that there are two parents in you. There are the parents of your biology, your genetic parents, and they give you life, that you have a propensity to engage that which is termed your environment according to your inherent qualities of your DNA, your genes. That is the one parent. That is the human parent. That is the parent of the body. But you have a greater parent and that is the parent of Point Zero, of that which is termed God, created from the Void. And if that says — wake up — that you are here to make known the unknown, and that the body is merely a garment and the brain a computer to create from the Void by collapsing energy into particle reality, it is your job to make known the unknown. And you have been a human being for ten and a half million years, and your trap is your emotional body and indeed that which is termed the body of your sensuality. That then says that you have two parents, one of God and one of genetics. Genetics gives you the body and the propensities for a personality. God gives you the Holy Spirit and a soul, that which has always been.

So who do you become in one lifetime? And those peoples that have stayed here and have studied have been bewildered at the voices they hear in their head that are the voices from the personality. And they begin to understand and to take responsibility for the choices they have made and to see that the son or daughter of God hath been a child within them that has allowed this to happen. And their choice has been clear: Learn to be the Observer and in the Observer you will feel nothing, because in feeling nothing is that which is termed the tribute that being the Observer is exactly what you are being.

When you are emotionless, you are that which is called bliss; thereby you are the heir apparent of God realized in life called Christ. And the mastership of this journey is to become that epic. And when you understand that emotions then are only to be experienced when God manifests in life and that the body then engage that life for a sensual experience, that only then do we have emotions that match the paradigm of the mind. When we understand that, we are masters awakened and the journey to Christhood is but a breath away.

The Awakening of the Observer and the New Life

So what have all these people been learning? They have been learning the greatest teaching that was ever taught, and that teaching was Behold God. It was not behold Christ as the only son of God. That would be foolish, and any entity of any mediocre intellect would be able to discern that there is certainly a flaw in the religious text, that God did not only have one child but that every child is God and that there was not only one son of God, that everyone is, and that Christ is merely that which is termed a paradigm that says that when we act and live according to the God within, rather than the personality within, are we then and can we claim that we are sons and daughters of the living God, and that it is this God that does the miracles, and it is that God that you are here in school to learn to become. So now the good news is that you are all the spawns of Point Zero.

Now listen. The voices you are going to hear in your head in that which is termed this Retreat[5] — and that is what this Retreat is about, moving from being red in the

---

5 Ramtha's disciplines of the Great Work are practical exercises that allow the student to experience the teachings firsthand. In this case the discipline is called "listening to the voices" and it is simply the act of quieting the body to become acutely aware and observe the continuous stream of thoughts we entertain in our head.

rainbow to listening to the chatter of social consciousness, body/mind consciousness — and you are going to ask yourself and I am going to remind you, who is listening? It is the "who" that I came here to reunite you with and not to dismiss. Those amongst you that have been working have been working to become the Observer, which in science and quantum mechanics it is called the Observer, but in religious mythology it is called the God within, the power of the anointed one.

THE PINNACLE OF THE GREAT WORK IS WHEN YOU LIVE IT

Now I have been teaching for twenty-one years in your time and counting, and you are that which is termed the epic apex of the teaching. There are people that have gotten the message. And what is the message? You are my greatest evolving group in this school, but do not let that sway you into an egotistical point of view to think that simply because you know this intellectually that you do not have to do the work to become, because to be able to say the words and to be able to recite them is a no-thing compared with the power to be able to ennoble them.

Now when I am finished with this work, there are many of you that are going to write many great scripts on the Great Work. But the ones of you who will be the pinnacle point of the Great Work are going to be those of you who did not simply intellectualize them into a facet of your biological personality, but will be those who enact them and indeed live them.

Now it is the year in the counting of your time — according to where you believe, either Gregorian or Julian calendar of time — it is the year 1998, and my time is at hand here. And so every moment that we are together, out of all of the rest of the days of your calendar year, let us make every moment pristine and valuable. And the way that we do that is to stay in the present, to live in the present of the moment, and not to jump ahead or to remember what was or to what you will do when this is over with, but to simply let go and to become that which is termed the word in a working principle. Then you can say when this event is over with, "My God, I wish it was never over because I literally allowed myself to become, which I have dared not to do before, and that I lived in the present."

47

Listen, God is the ruler of the present, the eternal Now. The personality is the ruler of time in what is called linear quadrant time. And if we are to be the lovers of linear time, then surely all you have to do is to go to the graveyard and read that which is termed what is carved upon the headstones to say, alas, these are the people who lived their life in linear time. And you also have to look at the headstone and say did they have the same dreams as me? Did they want to go to the same places? Did they want to be forever young? Did they want to be this? Did they try to do the right thing? Yes, but look where they are.

Now the masters are not in the graveyard; they are the eternal ones. There is no evidence, save the great ones historically, that they have lived because there is no evidence that they ever died. And archaeology, as we know, is built upon the precipice of carbon dating that which is termed bone and environmental fragments that determine a people in time and their particular habits. If a graveyard then a thousand years from now can be dug up from that which is termed — and let's hope that they are much more evolved than what is today, archaeologically speaking — can then determine who you were and what you ate and what you did, then we can look and say, well, obviously they knew something but they were incapable of exacting it into an environment that would allow they themselves to have a longer period of life.

What I represent, there is no evidence of us ever being here save what we put down into oral to stone to papyrus text, and the uncovering of ancient sites as the world changes, from that which is termed the hall of records in the paw of the Sphinx, that has already been found and will be made public in the next two years. And this will record the fabulous civilizations of 455,000 years ago, and from them we are going to learn about who was gifted with knowledge that was transcendent over flesh.

And you — you — already know that consciousness and energy creates the nature of reality. And that is not to say, nor can we argue the point, that the body and energy creates the nature of reality, because if we put it in that context, then we are going to run out of the biological patterns that dictate life. In other words, there is a death hormone that is being filled in the body through the pituitary gland. If we worship the body, we worship a limited time experience. However, if our consciousness is prone to that which is termed the supernatural quadrant of our being, that which science says is the Observer, that which can make plants react simply by our own presence, that we, according to science in how we observe the energy world around us, collapse our intent into particle collaboration, that collapse of cooperation of energy into particles is nothing more than reality. The body cannot do that because it in and of itself is a subject of the law of the Observer.

So obviously we look at the graveyard and we see people that were more beautiful than you would ever dream to be, and they are buried there, people who had dreams the same as you thought those dreams of yours were, and they are buried there, and so are their generations. And do you think there is anyone in the graveyard that is buried there that didn't have the same dreams as you do? The only thing that differs from your dreams and theirs is the technological advances that have been made since their death and while you are still living. But otherwise the principles are the same.

So now where is the evidence of the great ones? The evidence is they are not there; they are not buried. And if science is about tracking the historical evidence of man, then one of the great evidences would be the skeletal structure of the body preserved in time. But what about masters? Does it mean because they are not buried that somehow they didn't exist and that we can only say that they belong to myth? I tell you it is incorrect and is inconsistent, because quantum mechanics would suggest that if we understood the laws of physics and the simple point of the Observer, then those who do understand it would have never died because in the quantum world all potentials exist simultaneously.

And if indeed that it is possible for the human brain to conceive the concept of life in longevity — life without death, life in immortality, life forever young — if that can be conceived in the human brain, that certainly cannot live outside of the theorem that the Observer in the quantum field collapses reality, because if it does, then quantum mechanics is lacking yet a greater paradigm that would reconstruct that which is termed its whole constructs of mathematical and orientation of matter completely. That is to say then that quantum mechanics says the Observer determines reality, and of course reality then, it is only going to be relative to the capacity of the Observer to dream it. And what if the capacity of the Observer is to transcend biological — biological — clocks? No wonder God was deemed great amongst his prophets and that which talked about the kingdom of heaven, because they understood the science. And if it can be dreamed, it can be lived, and if it is lived, then the Observer is collapsing an immortal life.

Living As the Personality or the Observer

So the great teachings of this year is that this, our union together, is to recapture what the great ones knew and do know, and that is that man and woman are made up of two distinct powers. One is body/mind consciousness called the personality, and it is genetically and environmentally produced, the same as we would create a program on the computer; it is brain-based. The other is the Holy Spirit, the traveler in time that has never died, the one who you have never known, the one who views after death the life review and sees it with not only the feelings of shame and hurt but a new strength in making the next life even greater, because we never, ever advance beyond this life until we have owned what we have created here emotionally in the form of wisdom. And the day that we are finished with this life is the day that we can view life in a sense of detachment without emotion.

And who is to say then, and who is to argue and to what personality can argue then, what would be life without emotion? And I say to you, but have you ever lived the life from the Observer? And who are you to suggest from your emotional body that God hath no feeling for the whole creation to which God is? And who are you to say that it is nothing, when I say that those of us who have lived it can say that the point of true bliss and liberation is much more powerful and more real than that which is termed the chemical reactions in a biophysical body, such as pain, suffering, guilt, happiness, unhappiness, that which is termed security and insecurity. Those are all biological peptides that cause the body to react and nothing more. And when we live from that which is termed the Observer's point of view, then we, according to that which is termed the law of physics, choose to live from a higher echelon of thought, that then that thought becomes the law of our life and not our emotions.

And your challenge this year is to create a world, a life not based on the emotions, which are nothing more than the past of the dream, not to keep re-creating the past emotionally but to create new paradigms and new models for life that will not be created in emotion and will have nothing to do with body/mind consciousness but will have everything to do with the extraordinary mind that is beginning to know no barriers. And the last great teaching I will ever teach you will be about the Observer, and this is the year of the Observer. And now would you turn to your neighbor and explain to them what I have just taught you.[6]

I want you to remember everything you learn is not to make you sadder but to give you freedom. And every bit of knowledge you learn from me these days we are together seems that it is the undoing of the personality; it is supposed to be. But that is not to say that that which is termed who you are, extraneous from the personality, is not the quintessential beauty of what God is, because you are. I am not teaching you to be the divine within you and to say you must give up a life of sensual frivolity and then make a choice to a life of abstinence and austerity. If God is abstinence and austerity, it is too damn boring. Go back to your humanity.

God is rather that which is termed not only the giver of life, it is nature itself. God is not contained in the singular entity. Its life force is that which is termed the beauty of that which is termed the flowers that come from the fecund earth. The green, the lavender, and the rose that come from a drab and earth-colored seed that in the warmth of a spring morning can produce a flower of such extraordinary beauty and subtleness, and when it opens

---

6 It is important to participate and articulate the teaching even if you are by yourself. This process ensures the knowledge is recorded in long-term memory.

to exhale into the wind its fragrance, this is what God is. And God is the wind in midnight. God is that which is termed the waxing and the waning of the moon. It is that which is termed the ghostly apparitions of clouds at midnight over the moon. It is the stars, the children of the moon. It is the backdrop of forever. It is the smells. It is the light. It is the temperature. It is the beauty of all life. To say to you that these things are drab and boring is to say to a person who agrees that, no, you have never met nature nor have you understood its mysteries and its majesties and its beauties.

What I am going to teach you and what you will learn is that the personality that argues for its limitations, it argues for its place of altered ego. It argues for that which is termed its substantive individualism yet at once craving to be accepted. It argues for that which is limited, and yet the Observer that gives it life — the natural order of the body, its face, its intellect, that which is allowed a limited existence — also has the power of unlimited existence.

And if no one ever teaches you to dream the unlimited dream, if no one ever teaches you to breathe the breath of God's nostrils in spring, and if no one ever teaches you to look at a midnight sky and contemplate the concepts of forever, no one ever teaches you this, then you will be forever separated by God, its natural kingdom, its illustrious beauty, its intoxicating magic and enchantment. You will never know it. You are to learn that this is what the true nature of your being is, and that when you learn this you will know that the Lord God of your being is not trying to take you from life but to wake you up in the midst of it. And it is not one that argues for its limitation but barrels down the walls that limit you from expression.

So what you are going to learn about the Observer is not that dark, dank, monastic way of life. You never, ever will become a Christ when you abstain from life. I don't care who tells you what; no one ever ascends on abstinence. Abstinence is a natural evolution not of life itself but the personality that dictates the laws of life, that when we finally know God, we are no different than the wind in our hair and our laughter is no different than the voices in a quicksilver brook babbling under the shade of a willow. We are one and the same thing.

My message is not to say to you, give up your personality. Yes, that is the message, but my message is to say to you, give up what you conceive to be the highs in your life, and when you do, you will no longer be intoxicated, nor will you be addicted by the chemicals of feeling good. Feel-good is a biological/chemical place. God, if we are that, has to seek no place else to feel simply the marvelousness of our being. It is only our image that does this. And what would you rather be, limited by space and time and temperature or unlimited to be the whole without any need?

And the teaching is to say to all of you: Trust that when you learn these days that are coming the difference between your image and your Observer, you will have found God because that which listens to the voices in your head is that which we want to be. We would never want to be the voices. We would always want to be that which listens, because that is the godhead itself. And the teaching here is that what do we wish to be. We are in an Ancient School of Wisdom. If you don't want to hear this, you never had to be a part of this school.

It is taken for certitude that you have come here and learned to develop a basis and indeed a canon of knowledge to which you have not been able to have access to, and in the hopes and dreams and, of course, choices, that you could take this knowledge and apply it in your life to live a life that is fuller, richer, more unlimited, more joyful. So is the personality then the containment of all joy, all sensual feeling? Is indeed our altered ago that which is termed the glory of the intellect? Is that then what we would celebrate in the halls of intellectual knowledge? No, it isn't, for all of it pales to one who is unlimited and in that unlimitedness does not create intellectual philosophy but indeed creates intellectual reality.

If every philosopher that ever lived could experience his or her own theorems, if every philosopher that ever lived could experience his or her own myth, own legend, own philosophy, they would never have been remembered as a philosopher because they truly would have been able to experience what clearly they longed for intellectually. You are going to learn the difference.

Let it be understood from tonight forward, God is not boring but the personality is. And let it be understood tonight that the Observer is not limited, but the personality who argues is. If we must argue our place, we have already lost, for what we are we need not argue. If our freedom is the certitude of being, we need not fight for it. You never have to kill another person to be free. That would be the path of the victim. Freedom is self-ordained. If we have the freedom of thought, then we have the freedom of life. If we have to fight another for freedom, then we are simply saying that we are battling a war of the freedom of time in relation to our body, our personality. But no one can ever take from you in carnal existence the freedom to dream. And if you do not own that as the greatest apex of who you are, then you are already enslaved. War is about bodies; it is not about dreams. Remember that. So be it.

Truth is not anything to what I have to say. Truth isn't about what anyone has to say. That is hearsay. That is philosophy. It is theoretical paradigms. Truth is when we take the knowledge and have the experience ourself. Then and only then can we say that truth is, because it is a relative state of beingness. And you are going to learn the truth between the Observer and the personality, and once you learn that, then you too are going to have your different runners and your different disciplines to continue to perfect that. So be it.

Now have I told you that I love you? I want you to know that I love you greatly and always have and I always will.

And you are remarkable people, remarkable in ascertaining the morality of just beings, and marvelous that you dare to live outside of the boundaries of common thought. I love you, my beautiful people. Let us waste not one moment in this Retreat. Do not squander it in the smoking pit. Do not squander it in your automobiles. Participate at every moment, for these times, when you and I look as we do tonight, are drawing to an end. And you relish every moment because soon enough, I swear, this little time that we have dedicated to our own inner growth is going to come to an end and you will be thrust back into the world of cynicism and doubt, challenges and, of course, survival. So let us rejoice that we are together and make the most of every single moment and set doubt aside and let ourselves be free enough to prove that which is termed our only lack, tempered with the God within. So be it.

THE INITIATE IN PITCHED BATTLE

Now I am an old warrior and I can tell you that, you know, after a while in our march not everyone was so eager to run out there and draw the broadsword, because after a few battles what becomes chronic limitation is apathy. And you know what apathy is? It is those old soldiers that sit there and say they have done it all. They know what the battle is going to be. They know, they can predict, and yet when you rouse them to the surface to get out there and ride and march, they are the ones that don't feel so well — sixty-five years I saw this — and they are not so eager to go out there on the front because they say, "I have done this. I have done my bit in my own freedom. Why should I go out there and fight?" And what they are really saying is that "I made a few conquests and I lived through it."

And we know then that from taking that, that even the warriors of old who really fought that which is termed a hand-to-hand battle — they were in pitched battle is what they were — that for them to have done it once and to retire from it and say "I know what it is, I fought it, I can predict it" is really foolish. And nature would say you are foolish because we are evolving and changing, and so would be that which is termed the discipline in the school.

So that brings me back again to you, is that you came and you learned all the marvelous science. I want you to know you are greater than the old warriors of old who could sit there and say, "I know it all."

And of course we can already predict the skeptic's point of view that is going to say, "Well, just staying here a few extra days is not really anything. I mean, I could have done it. I could have done it, but I already knew what it was about." You know, those are the people that, you know, when the march moves on, they are the ones that the saffron dust settles on their eyelashes. So we are already gone beyond the hill and they are still sitting there saying, "Oh, I know what they are going to meet up ahead."

And some would argue that this is not about pitched battle. But, you know, in a way it is, and perhaps more than ever because I am actually asking you to battle and to conquer your body, your emotional body, your life. And what is the difference between meeting in battle an adversary?

You know, when the great Bel Shanai gave me the sword on the mountain when I was fourteen years of age — gave me a sword to beat up on the Unknown God — that it was the message that was a mystery. It says, "Go and conquer yourself." What am I going to do, turn the sword and cut my own head off? At fourteen years of age you have a distorted view of reality. No matter how the teenagers think in this audience, it is distorted. Yes, well, we are older and wiser; we can say that.

Well, I wanted to do battle with God. God sent me a woman who gave me a sword and said, "You conquer yourself." Well, the sword was very tangible. That which is termed my sword, as beautiful as it was, was a holy sword, but it was clear that those edges were so sharp they could cut the legs out from under a war-horse. So we are talking about conquering myself with a sword that was obviously meant for something else. Well, now we begin to understand that the something else was that in our reality exist the mirrors of our own self because otherwise, if they weren't ourself, they wouldn't be in our reality now, would they?

So who was going to survive in the creator and its reality when knowing all along that all the people in my life were also creators in the reality, and they were going to come up against creator to creator? And who was going to win? The one that was not their body. And God was going to side with that force and lop off the head of the very body that it inhabited. So you could say, well, this is nothing like that but, yes, it is, because it is easier to go into battle and kill someone else than it is to kill ourself. Correct? We could raze a towering, egotistical person down to ashes and delight in it. We could do that in my time, and we could do it to someone else because we are still confused with the concept that what is outside of us is not us, but in reality it is.

So now what do we do from pitched battle to the path of the master? It is the same thing except it is a little cleaner. That doesn't mean — that doesn't mean — that it is less dangerous and indeed it doesn't mean that it is less stressful. One whip of your sword in an analogical strike and your worries are over with that person and then you are onto the next one. Do you understand?

With that which is termed the altered ego, the emotional body, it is not so clear now, is it? It isn't so clear. But in fact the emotional body has in its vicinity, in its orbit, people who match exactly what it is, or otherwise it wouldn't keep running in the body. There is a magnetic connection. That is why we say that what we are is that we create reality, and the people, places, things, times, and events in our life represent our emotional body.

So how do we take then that which is termed a sword and defeat and conquer ourself in this new message? Well, it is what I have always said to you. First you have to address it in yourself. That is the enemy. "That emotion is my enemy," whether it is hypocrisy, stealing, lying, cheating, insecurity, diplomacy, guilt, the need to be wanted, which all can fall and flow into the format of insecurity. And there is a whole group of people that we put in our life to sort of prop that up. First we have to do away with them because when we do, we have addressed the emotional part of our body.

And, remember, we are not our body. It is a garment. And this body as garment was created specifically to do the job of a God that inhabits it through reality, and we collect upon us that which is termed the parasites of our own environment. And first we have to remove the parasite. What is going to happen after that? We are going to have a sore on our body, a swelling, and we are going to have it burst open and pus is going to run out of it, the draining of the corruption of the sore itself. And it is easy to put back onto us the parasite that will eat up the corruption, and it will suck out of us the poison. But what is it to remove the parasite and let the corruption burst and flow, because right after that the healing occurs. In fact the flowing of the corruption is the healing itself.

And what is the difference then in removing from our life, first going as a human being — Let's confront the problem, and you are the problem and thereby, whack, you are out of here. Then the body goes, "Woe is me. How could you have done that? I feel so bad." Well, then we have guilt and shame, and how dare you, and I was impetuous. And look at the consequences of that. And the body is in an emotional storm and you are having to sit there and deal with it, the whining widow, or widower; let's make it even here.

So who is the widow and the widower of our conquest? Our emotional body. And then we have to sit there and be the conqueror and say, "Suffer. You suffer." That is what you have to do. You can suffer, but you are not going to get any relief. And I can tell you that the greatest cure that takes us from the mundane part of our life is boredom. And I tell you, this emotional body is very smart. If it doesn't have any stimulus, it is going to get bored, and it is going to heal, and that sore is going to heal on the arm. I know that.

So now what is difficult about the march of the master is that we have to cleave our past from us, and it is about people, places, things, times, and events. And the next — the next — march is harder than ever because it is the emotional conquest that we must deal with. But only when this God has brought his army or her army under control are we going to be able to go to Shambhala. Not until then.

This work is harder than any march ever was because this is up close and personal. The enemy was impersonal, and all we had to fight then was our sense of bravery and confidence. But when it is your personality, when it is the very body you wear — when it is the very biological peptide, hormones, juices of the brain, the alchemy of the body — when that is that close to home we get blinded because we don't know how to differentiate self from the body. When we are looking at that wall, we are not really certain of our territory and we are not certain of the enemy, because the enemy at any moment could be the very personality to which we are making the judgments on.

And, you know, it is clever, but the one thing it will never do — it will never do — it will never permit you to destroy it. It will negotiate. That is why the image is a diplomat, and it is a clever one, and it knows how to resolve conflict without giving up anything. And if we are talking about a diplomat, we are talking about a diplomat not from God but from the emotional body itself. It will always resolve conflict in its favor; always will.

So then you are unsure of: "How am I addressing this? Am I addressing this from my emotional body or am I addressing this from my God?" This then is the problem. And that is why this battle is so heated and why the casualties are so great, that those who are victorious in it can be called legend and that they are revered as legend by those who participated in the battle. They can say, "My God, I could never become a master because I could never give up my emotional body. I couldn't give up my body. I couldn't give up my image. I couldn't give up my past. I couldn't give up my egotistical hold on my suffering that has bought my way to the present. I couldn't give that up because, my God, who would I be? It would be like laying down my shield, my battle-ax, my long sword, my short sword, and getting off of my steed and telling it to get out of here and then simply facing the enemy naked. How in the world could I do that? I can't do that. I can't even function in life with that because that is to say that suddenly I have amnesia." Exactly, exactly.

So that is why there are levels to this school. And in all the Ancient Schools of Wisdom there will always be remarkable people that come out of this, because even the least amongst you who then cry "Well, I have done this," you know, even in accomplishing the one battle gives you the smarts to create life better for yourself. But better for yourself, for whom, for the substantiation of your emotional body, your image, your body itself? It is going to give you a more comfortable life. It will.

And, you know, it may be a thousand more lifetimes before they come back and they say, "Well, I have been the most beautiful woman in the world several times. I have been the most handsome man in the world several times. I have been the richest man. I have been the richest woman. I have had freedom. I have been the most free of all people." All right now, don't you want the next step? And, you see, it may take a thousand lifetimes, people in this school, before they come back and understand this, because they are not finished with it. It is too good; you know, it feels too good.

And of course as the elder people in this audience will tell you, and if you go up and talk to anyone, they are the old ones. Don't look at an old woman and never think that she wasn't beautiful, because she was, and don't look at an old man in this audience whose hair is like the snow on the great mountain, whose beard is the same color and they are a little bent with age and their face has dropped with the weariness and the gravity of that weariness of their life, don't you ever think that that wasn't a young and virile man who thought he could conquer the world.

And you look at them in the audience and they have come to the end of their life and they are going "Everything that I was beautiful for and handsome for and everything that I was rich for and everything that I was virile for, well, I had so many women," or the women can say "I had men at my choosing because I was young and beautiful." Does that give them solace in their old age? Every one of them will say, "I was ready in my life for something else." What that means is that they are beyond youth and they are turning back and looking at it and saying what was this all for? And not one of them will ever say to you, "I wished that I was the same as I was then." What they will tell you is, "I wished I knew today what I knew when I was twenty years old." Correct?

And what do they represent in the psyche? Wisdom. They are the wise ones who say, "If I knew this at twenty years of age, I would never have aged, I will never have to fear death, and I would never have lost my beauty, and I could have incorporated in my vitality the wisdom that I know today. And if I know this I would never age another day, and I would never be sick, and I would have owned everything and would have been the blush of spring." That is the ideal.

Are you listening? You should, because if you are not, you are going to be one of them one of these days. Yes, you will. The graveyard bears it out. There is not a person in the cemetery that didn't think as you think in your arrogance. Not one, not one.

So in this battle — in this battle — it is hard because you are battling youth, hormones, peptides, body/mind consciousness, and your time is running out every day. Every day you see a new wrinkle, if you look really close, somewhere on your body. It is running out. It is running out. Those are the signs of the times. So the battle in this school is to suggest that though we have an advanced group here, that does not mean that every person in this group is here for the righteous intentions of the group itself. They are here to add a little spiritualism to their cause and effect of body/mind consciousness. I know that, and if you are older and wiser, you know that.

So what do you want to be? Do you want to be that? The body gives a great argument. People, places, things, times, and events will always argue for their limitations, what they perceive as self. And at the end of this, there will appear in your life a new being who will be none of those things. And then we uncover the greatest mystery there ever was, the Observer, and we begin to differentiate the Observer from the body and begin to define in the Observer a new state of feeling and a new power.

Entering the Place of No Words

This is the year that I have prophesied twenty years ago. This is the year that the Great Work comes into a magnetic proportion, which means we have built knowledge/discipline, knowledge/discipline, experience. This is the year that if you can define what could never be taught in words but could only be taught in relationship to that circle, that this is the year that you are going to start to move to the circle without words but with a lot of knowledge going in and intent going in, that if you can enter the circle and find the mystery of the true self, it is the true self that we as the masters of old incorporated in our life to bring about the new kingdom in our life.

When you can live as the Observer, you will manifest gold in your hand straightaway, you will manifest the most fantastic of dreams without ever going through the emotional body of editing, and then the experience of those dreams will be the frivolity and the joy, and now you understand why God has a body. And then you are going to experience it on the level of sensuality. And if you do that, you have found the holiest of holies, the sacred key to mastership and to Christhood.

And I swear to you, do not lose the momentum because there will come a day that the battle will be over with, and you walk out in that field the day you least expect it and you will go right to your cards, all of them. And you will start to laugh with such a joy, that if I put you in The Tank®, you would move right to the Void because you found the place of no words. And the appendages have fallen off, and the sore is oozing, and now it has that which is termed a scab on it and it is healing, and you are clean, and you know you have cleaned and you have worked it, and you have mastered people, places, things, times, and events and you are onto the greatest adventure that you could ever fathom, and because of that your life cannot end at sixty years old or seventy years old or eighty years old; that such an adventure is going to require at least at the onset two hundred years. So be it.

I accept the sword and I accept the adventure. So be it.

RAMTHA'S GLOSSARY

Analogical. Being analogical means living in the Now. It is the creative moment and is outside of time, the past, and the emotions.

Analogical mind. Analogical mind means one mind. It is the result of the alignment of primary consciousness and secondary consciousness, the Observer and the personality. The fourth, fifth, sixth, and seventh seals of the body are opened in this state of mind. The bands spin in opposite directions, like a wheel within a wheel, creating a powerful vortex that allows the thoughts held in the frontal lobe to coagulate and manifest.

Bands, the. The bands are the two sets of seven frequencies that surround the human body and hold it together. Each of the seven frequency layers of each band corresponds to the seven seals of seven levels of consciousness in the human body. The bands are the auric field that allow the processes of binary and analogical mind.

Binary mind. This term means two minds. It is the mind produced by accessing the knowledge of the human personality and the physical body without accessing our deep subconscious mind. Binary mind relies solely on the knowledge, perception, and thought processes of the neocortex and the first three seals. The fourth, fifth, sixth, and seventh seals remain closed in this state of mind.

Blue Body®. It is the body that belongs to the fourth plane of existence, the bridge consciousness, and the ultraviolet frequency band. The Blue Body® is the lord over the lightbody and the physical plane.

Blue Body® Dance. It is a discipline taught by Ramtha in which the students lift their conscious awareness to the consciousness of the fourth plane. This discipline allows the Blue Body® to be accessed and the fourth seal to be opened.

Blue Body® Healing. It is a discipline taught by Ramtha in which the students lift their conscious awareness to the consciousness of the fourth plane and the Blue Body® for the purpose of healing or changing the physical body.

Blue webs. The blue webs represent the basic structure at a subtle level of the physical body. It is the invisible skeletal structure of the physical realm vibrating at the level of ultraviolet frequency.

Body/mind consciousness. Body/mind consciousness is the consciousness that belongs to the physical plane and the human body.

Book of Life. Ramtha refers to the soul as the Book of Life, where the whole journey of involution and evolution of each individual is recorded in the form of wisdom.

C&E^{SM} **= R.** Consciousness and energy create the nature of reality.

C&E^{SM}**.** Abbreviation of Consciousness & Energy^{SM}. This is the service mark of the fundamental discipline of manifestation and the raising of consciousness taught in Ramtha's School of Enlightenment. Through this discipline the students learn to create an analogical state of mind, open up their higher seals, and create reality from the Void. A Beginning C&E^{SM} Workshop is the name of the introductory workshop for beginning students in which they learn the fundamental concepts and disciplines of Ramtha's teachings. The teachings of the Beginning C&E^{SM} Workshop can be found in *Ramtha: A Beginner's Guide to Creating Reality,* revised and expanded ed. (Yelm: JZK Publishing, a division of JZK, Inc., 2000), and in *Ramtha: Creating Personal Reality*, Video ed. (Yelm: JZK Publishing, a division of JZK, Inc., 1998).

Christwalk. The Christwalk is a discipline designed by Ramtha in which the student learns to walk very slowly being acutely aware. In this discipline the students learn to manifest, with each step they take, the mind of a Christ.

Consciousness. Consciousness is the child who was born from the Void's contemplation of itself. It is the essence and fabric of all being. Everything that exists originated in consciousness and manifested outwardly through its handmaiden energy. A stream of consciousness refers to the continuum of the mind of God.

Consciousness and energy. Consciousness and energy are the dynamic force of creation and are inextricably combined. Everything that exists originated in consciousness and manifested through the modulation of its energy impact into mass.

Disciplines of the Great Work. Ramtha's School of Ancient Wisdom is dedicated to the Great Work. The disciplines of the Great Work practiced in Ramtha's School of Enlightenment are all designed in their entirety by Ramtha. These practices are powerful initiations where the student has the opportunity to apply and experience firsthand the teachings of Ramtha.

Emotional body. The emotional body is the collection of past emotions, attitudes, and electrochemical patterns that make up the brain's neuronet and define the human personality of an individual. Ramtha describes it as the seduction of the unenlightened. It is the reason for cyclical reincarnation.

Emotions. An emotion is the physical, biochemical effect of an experience. Emotions belong to the past, for they are the expression of experiences that are already known and mapped in the neuropathways of the brain.

Energy. Energy is the counterpart of consciousness. All consciousness carries with it a dynamic energy impact, radiation, or natural expression of itself. Likewise, all forms of energy carry with it a consciousness that defines it.

Enlightenment. Enlightenment is the full realization of the human person, the attainment of immortality, and unlimited mind. It is the result of raising the kundalini energy sitting at the base of the spine to the seventh seal that opens the dormant parts of the brain. When the energy penetrates the lower cerebellum and the midbrain, and the subconscious mind is opened, the individual experiences a blinding flash of light called enlightenment.

Evolution. Evolution is the journey back home from the slowest levels of frequency and mass to the highest levels of consciousness and Point Zero.

Fieldwork^SM. Fieldwork^SM is one of the fundamental disciplines of Ramtha's School of Enlightenment. The students are taught to create a symbol of something they want to know and experience and draw it on a paper card. These cards are placed with the blank side facing out on the fence rails of a large field. The students blindfold themselves and focus on their symbol, allowing their body to walk freely to find their card through the application of the law of consciousness and energy and analogical mind.

Fifth plane. The fifth plane of existence is the plane of superconsciousness and x-ray frequency. It is also known as the Golden Plane or paradise.

Fifth seal. This seal is the center of our spiritual body that connects us to the fifth plane. It is associated with the thyroid gland and with speaking and living the truth without dualism.

First plane. It refers to the material or physical plane. It is the plane of the image consciousness and Hertzian frequency. It is the slowest and densest form of coagulated consciousness and energy.

First seal. The first seal is associated with the reproductive organs, sexuality, and survival.

First three seals. The first three seals are the seals of sexuality, pain and suffering, and controlling power. These are the seals commonly at play in all of the complexities of the human drama.

Fourth plane. The fourth plane of existence is the realm of the bridge consciousness and ultraviolet frequency. This plane is described as the plane of Shiva, the destroyer of the old and creator of the new. In this plane, energy is not yet split into positive and negative polarity. Any lasting changes or healing of the physical body must be changed first at the level of the fourth plane and the Blue Body®. This plane is also called the Blue Plane, or the plane of Shiva.

Fourth seal. The fourth seal is associated with unconditional love and the thymus gland. When this seal is activated, a hormone is released that maintains the body in perfect health and stops the aging process.

God. Ramtha's teachings are an exposition of the statement, "You are God." Humanity is described as the forgotten Gods. God is different from the Void. God is the point of awareness that sprang from the Void contemplating itself. It is consciousness and energy exploring and making known the unknown potentials of the Void. It is the omnipotent and omnipresent essence of all creation.

God within. It is the Observer, the great self, the primary consciousness, the Spirit, the God within the human person.

God/man. The full realization of a human being.

God/woman. The full realization of a human being.

Gods. The Gods are technologically advanced beings from other star systems who came to Earth 455,000 years ago. These Gods manipulated the human race genetically, mixing and modifying our DNA with theirs. They are responsible for the evolution of the neocortex and used the human race as a subdued work force. Evidence of these events is recorded in the Sumerian tablets and artifacts. This term is also used to describe the true identity of humanity, the forgotten Gods.

Golden body. It is the body that belongs to the fifth plane, superconsciousness, and x-ray frequency.

Great Work. The Great Work is the practical application of the knowledge of the Schools of Ancient Wisdom. It refers to the disciplines by which the human person becomes enlightened and is transmuted into an immortal, divine being.

Hierophant. A hierophant is a master teacher who is able to manifest what they teach and initiate their students into such knowledge.

Hyperconsciousness. Hyperconsciousness is the consciousness of the sixth plane and gamma ray frequency.

Infinite Unknown. It is the frequency band of the seventh plane of existence and ultraconsciousness.

Involution. Involution is the journey from Point Zero and the seventh plane to the slowest and densest levels of frequency and mass.

JZ Knight. JZ Knight is the only person appointed by Ramtha to channel him. Ramtha refers to JZ as his beloved daughter. She was Ramaya, the eldest of the children given to Ramtha during his lifetime.

Kundalini. Kundalini energy is the life force of a person that descends from the higher seals to the base of the spine at puberty. It is a large packet of energy reserved for human evolution, commonly pictured as a coiled serpent that sits at the base of the spine. This energy is different from the energy coming out of the first three seals responsible for sexuality, pain and suffering, power, and victimization. It is commonly described as the sleeping serpent or the sleeping dragon. The journey of the kundalini energy to the crown of the head is called the journey of enlightenment. This journey takes place when this serpent wakes up and starts to split and dance around the spine, ionizing the spinal fluid and changing its molecular structure. This action causes the opening of the midbrain and the door to the subconscious mind.

Life force. The life force is the Father/Mother, the Spirit, the breath of life within the person that is the platform from which the person creates its illusions, imagination, and dreams.

Life review. It is the review of the previous incarnation that occurs when the person reaches the third plane after death. The person gets the opportunity to be the Observer, the actor, and the recipient of its own actions. The unresolved issues from that lifetime that emerge at the life or light review set the agenda for the next incarnation.

Light, the. The light refers to the third plane of existence.

Lightbody. It is the same as the radiant body. It is the body that belongs to the third plane of conscious awareness and the visible light frequency band.

List, the. The List is the discipline taught by Ramtha where the student gets to write a list of items they desire to know and experience and then learn to focus on it in an analogical state of consciousness. The List is the map used to design, change, and reprogram the neuronet of the person. It is the tool that helps to bring meaningful and lasting changes in the person and their reality.

Make known the unknown. This phrase expresses the original divine mandate given to the Source consciousness to manifest and bring to conscious awareness all of the infinite potentials of the Void. This statement represents the basic intent that inspires the dynamic process of creation and evolution.

Mind. Mind is the product of streams of consciousness and energy acting on the brain creating thought forms, holographic segments, or neurosynaptic patterns called memory. The streams of consciousness and energy are what keep the brain alive. They are its power source. A person's ability to think is what gives them a mind.

Mind of God. The mind of God comprises the mind and wisdom of every lifeform that ever lived on any dimension, in any time, or that ever will live on any planet, any star, or region of space.

Mirror consciousness. When Point Zero imitated the act of contemplation of the Void it created a mirror reflection of itself, a point of reference that made the exploration of the Void possible. It is called mirror consciousness or secondary consciousness. See **Self.**

Monkey-mind. Monkey-mind refers to the flickering, swinging mind of the personality.

Mother/Father Principle. It is the source of all life, the Father, the eternal Mother, the Void. In Ramtha's teachings, the Source and God the creator are not the same. God the creator is seen as Point Zero and primary consciousness but not as the Source, or the Void, itself.

Name-field. The name-field is the name of the large field where the discipline of Fieldwork^{SM} is practiced.

Observer. It refers to the Observer responsible for collapsing the particle/wave of quantum mechanics. It represents the great self, the Spirit, primary consciousness, the God within the human person.

Outrageous. Ramtha uses this word in a positive way to express something or someone who is extraordinary and unusual, unrestrained in action, and excessively bold or fierce.

People, places, things, times, and events. These are the main areas of human experience to which the personality is emotionally attached. These areas represent the past of the human person and constitute the content of the emotional body.

Personality, the. *See* **Emotional body.**

Plane of Bliss. It refers to the plane of rest where souls get to plan their next incarnations after their life reviews. It is also known as heaven and paradise where there is no suffering, no pain, no need or lack, and where every wish is immediately manifested.

Plane of demonstration. The physical plane is also called the plane of demonstration. It is the plane where the person has the opportunity to demonstrate its creative potentiality in mass and witness consciousness in material form in order to expand its emotional understanding.

Point Zero. It refers to the original point of awareness created by the Void through its act of contemplating itself. Point Zero is the original child of the Void, the birth of consciousness.

Primary consciousness. It is the Observer, the great self, the God within the human person.

Ram. Ram is a shorter version of the name Ramtha. Ramtha means the Father.

Ramaya. Ramtha refers to JZ Knight as his beloved daughter. She was Ramaya, the first one to become Ramtha's adopted child during his lifetime. Ramtha found Ramaya abandoned on the steppes of Russia. Many people gave their children to Ramtha during the march as a gesture of love and highest respect; these children were to be raised in the House of the Ram. His children grew to the great number of 133 even though he never had offspring of his own blood.

Ramtha (etymology). The name of Ramtha the Enlightened One, Lord of the Wind, means the Father. It also refers to the Ram who descended from the mountain on what is known as the Terrible Day of the Ram. "It is about that in all antiquity. And in ancient Egypt, there is an avenue dedicated to the Ram, the great conqueror. And they were wise enough to understand that whoever could walk down the avenue of the Ram could conquer the wind." The word Aram, the name of Noah's grandson, is formed from the Aramaic noun Araa — meaning earth, landmass — and the word Ramtha, meaning high. This Semitic name echoes Ramtha's descent from the high mountain, which began the great march.

Runner. A runner in Ramtha's lifetime was responsible for bringing specific messages or information. A master teacher has the ability to send runners to other people that manifest their words or intent in the form of an experience or an event.

Second plane. It is the plane of existence of social consciousness and the infrared frequency band. It is associated with pain and suffering. This plane is the negative polarity of the third plane of visible light frequency.

Second seal. This seal is the energy center of social consciousness and the infrared frequency band. It is associated with the experience of pain and suffering and is located in the lower abdominal area.

Secondary consciousness. When Point Zero imitated the act of contemplation of the Void it created a mirror reflection of itself, a point of reference that made the exploration of the Void possible. It is called mirror consciousness or secondary consciousness. See **Self.**

Self, the. The self is the true identity of the human person different from the personality. It is the transcendental aspect of the person. It refers to the secondary consciousness, the traveler in a journey of involution and evolution making known the unknown.

Sending-and-receiving. Sending-and-receiving is the name of the discipline taught by Ramtha in which the student learns to access information using the faculties of the midbrain to the exclusion of sensory perception. This discipline develops the student's psychic ability of telepathy and divination.

Seven seals. The seven seals are powerful energy centers that constitute seven levels of consciousness in the human body. The bands are the way in which the physical body is held together according to these seals. In every human being there is energy spiraling out of the first three seals or centers. The energy pulsating out of the first three seals manifests itself respectively as sexuality, pain, or power. When the upper seals are unlocked, a higher level of awareness is activated.

Seventh plane. The seventh plane is the plane of ultraconsciousness and the Infinite Unknown frequency band. This plane is where the journey of involution began. This plane was created by Point Zero when it imitated the act of contemplation of the Void and the mirror or secondary consciousness was created. A plane of existence or dimension of space and time exists between two points of consciousness. All the other planes were created by slowing down the time and frequency band of the seventh plane.

Seventh seal. This seal is associated with the crown of the head, the pituitary gland, and the attainment of enlightenment.

Shiva. The Lord God Shiva represents the Lord of the Blue Plane and the Blue Body®. Shiva is not used in reference to a singular deity from Hinduism. It is rather the representation of a state of consciousness that belongs to the fourth plane, the ultraviolet frequency band, and the opening of the fourth seal. Shiva is neither male nor female. It is an androgynous being, for the energy of the fourth plane has not yet been split into positive and negative polarity. This is an important distinction from the traditional Hindu representation of Shiva as a male deity who has a wife. The tiger skin at its feet, the trident staff, and the sun and the moon at the level of the head represent the mastery of this body over the first three seals of consciousness. The kundalini energy is pictured as fiery energy shooting from the base of the spine through the head. This is another distinction from some Hindu representations of Shiva with the serpent energy coming out at the level of the fifth seal or throat. Another symbolic image of Shiva is the long threads of dark hair and an abundance of pearl necklaces, which represent its richness of experience owned into wisdom. The quiver and bow and arrows are the agent by which Shiva shoots its powerful will and destroys imperfection and creates the new.

Sixth plane. The sixth plane is the realm of hyperconsciousness and the gamma ray frequency band. In this plane the awareness of being one with the whole of life is experienced.

Sixth seal. This seal is associated with the pineal gland and the gamma ray frequency band. The reticular formation that filters and veils the knowingness of the subconscious mind is opened when this seal is activated. The opening of the brain refers to the opening of this seal and the activation of its consciousness and energy.

Social consciousness. It is the consciousness of the second plane and the infrared frequency band. It is also called the image of the human personality and the mind of the first three seals. Social consciousness refers to the collective consciousness of human society. It is the collection of thoughts, assumptions, judgments, prejudices, laws, morality, values, attitudes, ideals, and emotions of the fraternity of the human race.

Soul. Ramtha refers to the soul as the Book of Life, where the whole journey of involution and evolution of the individual is recorded in the form of wisdom.

Subconscious mind. The seat of the subconscious mind is the lower cerebellum or reptilian brain. This part of the brain has its own independent connections to the frontal lobe and the whole of the body and has the power to access the mind of God, the wisdom of the ages.

Superconsciousness. This is the consciousness of the fifth plane and the x-ray frequency band.

Tahumo. Tahumo is the discipline taught by Ramtha in which the student learns the ability to master the effects of the natural environment — cold and heat — on the human body.

Tank field. It is the name of the large field with the labyrinth that is used for the discipline of The Tank®.

Tank®, The. It is the name given to the labyrinth used as part of the disciplines of Ramtha's School of Enlightenment. The students are taught to find the entry to this labyrinth blindfolded and move through it focusing on the Void without touching the walls or using the eyes or the senses. The objective of this discipline is to find, blindfolded, the center of the labyrinth or a room designated and representative of the Void.

Third plane. This is the plane of conscious awareness and the visible light frequency band. It is also known as the light plane and the mental plane. When the energy of the Blue Plane is lowered down to this frequency band, it splits into positive and negative polarity. It is at this point that the soul splits into two, giving origin to the phenomenon of soulmates.

Third seal. This seal is the energy center of conscious awareness and the visible light frequency band. It is associated with control, tyranny, victimization, and power. It is located in the region of the solar plexus.

Thought. Thought is different from consciousness. The brain processes a stream of consciousness, modifying it into segments — holographic pictures — of neurological, electrical, and chemical prints called thoughts. Thoughts are the building blocks of mind.

Twilight®. This term is used to describe the discipline taught by Ramtha in which the students learn to put their bodies in a catatonic state similar to deep sleep, yet retaining their conscious awareness.

Twilight® Visualization Process. It is the process used to practice the discipline of the List or other visualization formats.

Ultraconsciousness. It is the consciousness of the seventh plane and the Infinite Unknown frequency band. It is the consciousness of an ascended master.

Unknown God. The Unknown God was the single God of Ramtha's ancestors, the Lemurians. The Unknown God also represents the forgotten divinity and divine origin of the human person.

Upper four seals. The upper four seals are the fourth, fifth, sixth, and seventh seals.

Void, the. The Void is defined as one vast nothing materially, yet all things potentially. *See* **Mother/Father Principle.**

Yellow brain. The yellow brain is Ramtha's name for the neocortex, the house of analytical and emotional thought. The reason why it is called the yellow brain is because the neocortices were colored yellow in the original two-dimensional, caricature-style drawing Ramtha used for his teaching on the function of the brain and its processes. He explained that the different aspects of the brain in this particular drawing are exaggerated and colorfully highlighted for the sake of study and understanding. This specific drawing became the standard tool used in all the subsequent teachings on the brain.

Yeshua ben Joseph. Ramtha refers to Jesus Christ by the name Yeshua ben Joseph, following the Jewish traditions of that time.

Fig. A: The Seven Seals:
Seven Levels of Consciousness in the Human Body

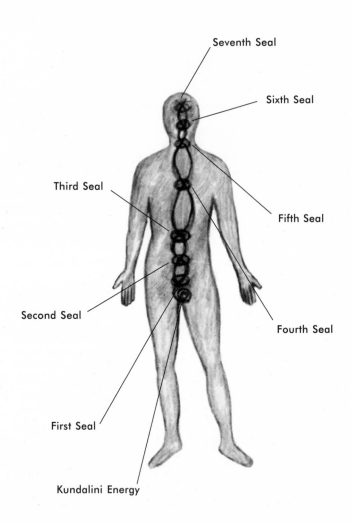

Seventh Seal

Sixth Seal

Third Seal

Fifth Seal

Second Seal

Fourth Seal

First Seal

Kundalini Energy

FIG. B: SEVEN LEVELS OF CONSCIOUSNESS AND ENERGY

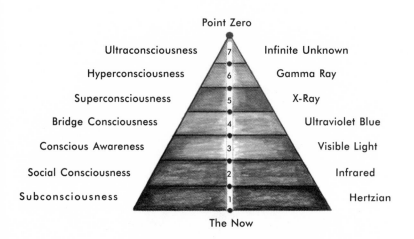

Point Zero

Ultraconsciousness	7	Infinite Unknown
Hyperconsciousness	6	Gamma Ray
Superconsciousness	5	X-Ray
Bridge Consciousness	4	Ultraviolet Blue
Conscious Awareness	3	Visible Light
Social Consciousness	2	Infrared
Subconsciousness	1	Hertzian

The Now

FIG. C: THE BRAIN

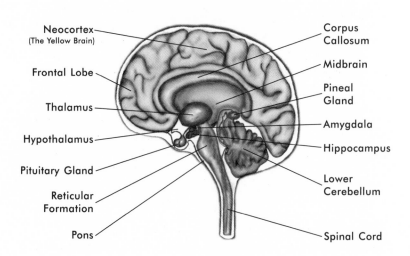

Neocortex
(The Yellow Brain)

Frontal Lobe

Thalamus

Hypothalamus

Pituitary Gland

Reticular Formation

Pons

Corpus Callosum

Midbrain

Pineal Gland

Amygdala

Hippocampus

Lower Cerebellum

Spinal Cord

Fig. D: Binary Mind — Living the Image

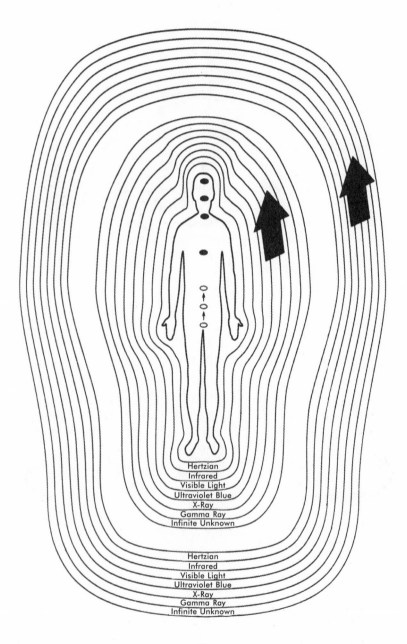

FIG. E: ANALOGICAL MIND — LIVING IN THE NOW

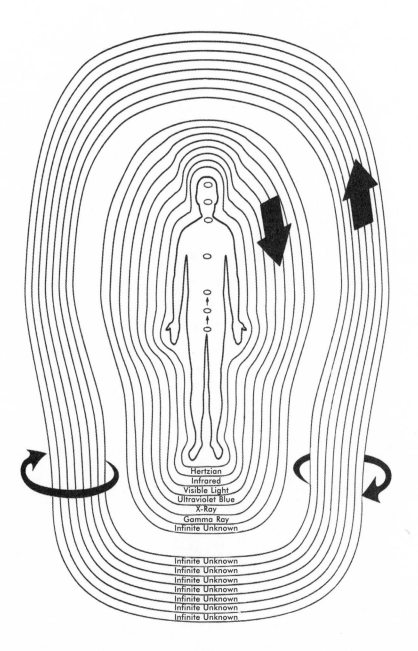

Ramtha's School of Enlightenment,
THE SCHOOL OF ANCIENT WISDOM

A Division of JZK, Inc.
P.O. Box 1210
Yelm, Washington 98597
360.458.5201
800.347.0439
www.ramtha.com
www.jzkpublishing.com